The Joy

of Christmas

The Joy
of Christmas

Martin H. Manser
Andrew Bianchi

Copyright © 2003 by Barnes & Noble, Inc.

2003 Barnes & Noble Books

ISBN 0-7607-4500-5

Printed and bound in the United States

Book design by Lundquist Design, New York

MC 9 8 7 6 5 4 3 2 1

Introduction

There's something completely different about Christmas. Our ordinary selves seem to be taken over as the big day approaches. We get more and more frantic, our to-do lists grow longer, and we all rush around in ever-decreasing circles.

When the publishers asked me to compile a book of short readings and quotations on this great theme, I wasn't sure I could do it justice. After all, Christmas represents the most amazing fact ever: God taking on our humanity. The message seems too good to be true. It seems too miraculous. And yet this message is meant to affect us, not only at Christmas but on every other day of our lives as well.

I began to list aspects of this great theme: giving, joy, family, worship, goodwill to all, celebration, hope, peace. . . . I called on my good friend Andy Bianchi to help me explore what

Christmas means, to unravel some of its wonders, to touch on its uniqueness. We hope that as you dip into this little book, you will see afresh what Christmas is really all about.

Martin H. Manser

To perceive Christmas through its wrapping becomes more difficult every year.

E. B. White

Why on Earth are Those Angels on Earth?

I was waiting for a bus the other day. Then, as soon as the one I wanted came, two more appeared. It's a great mystery. Experts, whose miserable job it seems is to take the intrigue out of life, tell us this happens because the first one is continually stopping to pick up passengers; the others, with no one to collect, go more quickly and eventually catch up.

These same experts have never explained why angels—like buses—appear in bursts. For centuries before Jesus was born, there was scarcely a sniff of them. Suddenly, they are jumping about all over the place. Mary, Zechariah, Joseph, and the shepherds are all quietly minding their own business when they each get a celestial visit. Then without warning they disappear, and are seldom seen again. Why?

It might be that, because they frighten humans so much, God decides to use them sparingly—saving them for special occasions, when the danger of causing shock is far outweighed by the need to point out that something important is going on. Perhaps that's why so many were rushing around two thousand years ago. Or maybe they were so fascinated by the idea of God coming down and living as a baby, they just had to see for themselves what was happening on Planet Earth. And when they did— as the shepherds could testify—nothing could contain their happiness.

SUDDENLY A GREAT COMPANY OF THE HEAVENLY HOST APPEARED WITH THE ANGEL, PRAISING GOD . . .

Luke 2:13

Angels from the realms of
  glory,
Wing your flight o'er all the
  earth;
Ye who sang creation's story,
Now proclaim Messiah's birth.

James Montgomery

Its visits
Like those of angels, short, and
  far between.

Robert Blair

Even angels long to look into
these things.

1 Peter 1:12

Angels we have heard on high,
Sweetly singing o'er the plains
And the mountains in reply
Echoing their joyous strains.
Gloria, In Excelsius Deo.

Traditional French carol
translated by James Chadwick

Mary 1, Zechariah 0

"Haven't seen you for a while, Gabriel. Been busy?"

"Busy? These last six months I've done nothing but carry birth announcements to Earth. Strange lot, those humans. However much I try not to upset them, they always seem to get frightened when I turn up."

"Have you tried looking at yourself in the mirror?"

"What? Don't try to be funny. And the other thing is, you can never predict how they are going to react to what you tell them—when they've finally stopped shaking with fear that is.

"Take the last two people I saw for instance. One was a priest. Knew his Bible back to front. Lifetime of service. Been there, done that, bought the robe. Devout. Genuine. I'd be surprised if you could find a better man anywhere in Israel. He and his wife had been trying for a baby for years. I couldn't wait to see his face light up with excitement.

"Then there was this other one. A young woman. Well, a girl really. Engaged to be married she was. I had to tell her she was going to have a baby that was going to be conceived by God's Holy Spirit. I was rather dreading it, to be honest. It's not every day you have to tell a single woman she is going to give birth to a child in such mysterious circumstances. Can you imagine trying to explain that to her parents, let alone her fiancé? The strange thing was that only one of them believed me."

"The professional?"

"No, the young woman."

No man is poor who has had a
godly mother.

Abraham Lincoln

Blessed are you among women . . .

Luke 1:42

Mary said: My soul glorifies
the Lord and my spirit rejoices in
God my Savior.

Luke 1:46-47

Mary was that Mother mild,
Jesus Christ her little Child.

Cecil Frances Alexander

Slowing Down

Yes, it's Christmas time again. I'm running late. I know I should have mailed all the presents to friends around the world. But, as usual, I'm running late. Yes, that's it, I'm running. I never seem to stop. Yes, there was that newspaper article on "A hundred ways to slow down"; the only trouble was, I never had time to act on them. I speed-read the article, and then dashed on to the next thing.

I remember all the movies about spending time with my kids and stopping to pass the time of day with folks, yet I'm wrapped up in myself. There's that old lady down the street whose husband died last year. Who will look after her this Christmas?

Lord, help me to see you in all this Christmas "stuff." Help me to remember you, to turn aside from myself and my world and think of you, for even a few minutes, this Christmas time.

If I do turn to you, I know that somehow (and I'm never quite sure how) you will make me new inside. Give me the courage and strength to bring myself, just as I am, to your infinite greatness. Help me to be humble enough to come afresh and worship you, Lord Jesus, the new-born king.

Now what present can I get for my wife?

JESUS KNOWS WE MUST COME APART
AND REST AWHILE, OR ELSE WE MAY
JUST PLAIN COME APART.

Vance Havner

LIFE LIVED AMIDST TENSION AND
  BUSYNESS NEEDS LEISURE.
LEISURE THAT RE-CREATES AND
  RENEWS.
LEISURE SHOULD BE A TIME TO THINK
  NEW THOUGHTS, NOT PONDER OLD
  ILLS.

C. Neil Strait

SAGES, LEAVE YOUR CONTEMPLATIONS,
BRIGHTER VISIONS BEAM AFAR;
SEEK THE GREAT DESIRE OF NATIONS;
YE HAVE SEEN HIS NATAL STAR:
COME AND WORSHIP,
WORSHIP CHRIST, THE NEW-BORN
  KING.

James Montgomery

A Festive
Nightmare

Last year it happened twice. The year before that once, and now it's happened again. However hard I try, however much I anticipate it, I am always caught out by that most dreadful of Christmas nightmares—receiving a card or present from someone who was not on my outgoing list. When it happens, only two options are available. One is to reply in kind as quickly as possible; the other is to lie low and resume reciprocation the following year.

Why am I caught up in this web of exchange? Why is Christmas giving so often reduced to a guessing game in which the only thing that matters is not to be caught out? Is it the fault of the Wise Men, who, when presented with the most valuable gift the world has ever known, gave the relatively insignificant gifts of gold, incense, and myrrh? Were their gifts those of competition or of appreciation? Were they caught up in my cycle of tit-for-tat giving, unable to accept the free gift of a baby boy? I like to think they gave because they knew what the gift really meant, rather than to curry favor with the giver. They understood that God had given of Himself not because *He had to*, but because *He wanted to*. So they in turn gave of their wealth, not because of some competitive urge, but because they were able to recognize divine kindness. I wonder whether we struggle at Christmas because we live in a world that is no longer comfortable with this idea of free grace?

Oh what a gift! What a wonderful gift!

Pat Uhl Howard

The only gift is a portion of thyself.

Ralph Waldo Emerson

Then they opened their treasures and presented him with gifts of gold and of incense and of myrrh.

Matthew 2:11

Santa Claus

What child enjoys writing thank-you letters? What parent has not had to nag a son or daughter a thousand times to sit down with pen and paper and tell unknown aunts how pleased they were (for the third Christmas in a row) to receive the very pair of socks they had been hoping for?

Yet there is one type of letter all children love to write. A letter to Santa Claus. A letter of hope. A letter whose composition fills the heart with excitement and anticipation. Even those disappointed last year apply themselves to the task with enthusiasm, as fresh dreams pass before their minds' eyes. The bike, the scooter, the doll, the computer game, the video, the pony. The list is as long as imagination will let it be. Where parents have already said, "We'll see," "I'm not sure if we can afford that," or countless other excuses, Santa will never say "No."

What adult—what parent—would begrudge a child Santa Claus? This kindly man offers them the chance to live with an exciting dream locked up in their heart. He gives them the possibility of appealing to a figure whose kindness knows no bounds or limits. The opportunity to communicate with someone whose sole reason for existence is to bring happiness to others. He brings the gift of simply being a child whose heart and soul are still uncluttered by the cynicism and hardness of the world. And isn't this perhaps the greatest gift Santa can bring any hopeful boy or girl?

God isn't a Santa Claus, but He, too, longs to give good gifts to all His children, if they will only ask Him.

SANTA CLAUS IS THE FAIRYTALE THAT COMES ALIVE WHEN WE ARE OLD ENOUGH TO UNDERSTAND THE MAGIC OF OUR PARENTS' LOVE.

Ina Hughes

ALAS! HOW DREARY THE WORLD WOULD BE IF THERE WERE NO SANTA CLAUS!

Francis Church

Dreaming of a White Christmas?

I have just finished looking at a map of America issued by the National Oceanic and Atmospheric Administration. Using statistical analysis from past years, it attempts to give an answer to that most pressing of Christmas questions: Will we have a white Christmas? Sadly, it looks as though the chances are slim for the majority of us this year. Not only that, but for many Americans, the white Christmases "we used to know" have never taken place. And what about those people who live in Australia or South America? I wonder how many of them have ever seen snow—let alone on December 25th?

In greeting cards, in advertising, and in store decorations throughout our land, the dream of a white Christmas continues—oblivious to the sober voice of climatological reason.

And I say, "Long live the dream."

For what better captures the joy of the occasion than a snowball fight? What better captures our sense of wonder than the pure, dazzling simplicity of snow? What better reminds us of our individuality than the infinitely variable patterns of snowflakes? And on those bitter nights when the cold stare of the moon reflects down onto the hard and silent snow, is it not true that the protective warmth of our homes reminds us of those loving arms of God as He longs to take us in His arms and shelter us from life's storm? Long live the dream!

In the bleak midwinter,
Frosty wind made moan,
Earth stood hard as iron.
Water like a stone;
Snow had fallen, snow on snow,
Snow on snow,
In the bleak midwinter,
Long ago.

Christina Rossetti

I have often thought, says Sir
Roger, it happens very well that
Christmas should fall out in the
Middle of Winter.

Joseph Addison

What is Christmas without snow?

R. S. Thomas

I'm dreaming of a white Christmas
Just like the ones I used to know.

Irving Berlin

Stand by Your Woman

If an angelic visit is a sign that God thinks someone is special, then the best of the Bethlehem bunch by a long way is Joseph. On no fewer than three occasions does a heavenly messenger confront him. You can almost imagine him, third time round, sighing, "Oh, it's you again. Pull up a chair, I'm just changing a diaper. Be with you in a minute."

Of course, Mary is the one who gets all the good publicity. She is the one revered by countless millions. She is the one with statues and altars and the like. It's Mary who is celebrated in carols and churches. Mother and child and all that. But what recognition does poor Joseph get? Hardly any. And yet, as we read the Gospel accounts, he comes across as a very special person. Mr. Dependable—a man of trust. A man of obedience. A man of love.

After all, imagine your fiancée coming to you with some strange story explaining the increased size of her belly. Even if you had the courage to believe her, what would your friends say? How would you tell that to the guys and expect them to keep a straight face? Every time Joseph went out with his boy, people would turn and stare, their eyes full of patronizing pity and their lips full of hearsay and gossip.

In giving birth to Jesus, Mary did an amazing thing. A thing no human had ever done. But let's not forget that Joseph did an amazing thing too. He stood by his woman.

B ECAUSE JOSEPH HER HUSBAND WAS
A RIGHTEOUS MAN AND DID NOT WANT
TO EXPOSE HER TO PUBLIC DISGRACE,
HE HAD IN MIND TO DIVORCE HER
QUIETLY.

Matthew 1:19

H E WAS THE SON, SO IT WAS
THOUGHT, OF JOSEPH . . .

Luke 3:23

Gift Wrapped

Sometimes I wonder why we bother giving presents to very young babies at Christmas. We're lucky if they play with the gift for more than a minute before settling down to the real excitement of messing around with the wrapping paper. Indeed, one Christmas, I'm going to buy all the babies I know presents that I would like for myself. Then I'll put each one on the floor surrounded by a sea of snowmen, bells, and angels. While they are busy crinkling and crackling the brightly colored paper, I plan to sneak in and reclaim the gifts for myself. I'll be happy, and they'll be none the wiser. I'll have to be quick, though.

But sooner or later, babies learn what the rest of us know. It's what's inside that counts. However cute the teddy bears, however cherub like the angels, however white the snowflakes, we learn to go beyond all that to the present itself.

We don't know anything about the appearance, the wrapping, of that middle-eastern baby. Was he cute? What was the color of his hair? Were his eyes, when he wasn't snuggled up in Mary's or Joseph's arms, blue, brown, or hazel? Was he chubby? Was he wrinkly? Hairy? Did he wriggle? We don't know for the simple reason that it doesn't matter. Only one thing mattered—God had wrapped Himself in our humanity.

How He's done it is beyond me. I can't understand it, and I suppose I never will. But then, being a man, I still haven't worked out how to wrap a present decently either.

VEILED IN FLESH THE GODHEAD SEE!
HAIL, THE INCARNATE DEITY!

Charles Wesley

FILLING THE WORLD HE LIES IN A
MANGER.

St. Augustine

QUIET HE LIES
WHOSE VIGOR HURLED A UNIVERSE.

Luci Shaw

Happy Birthday!

It was another bad year for me. I forgot two birthdays. Both of them were family members, and don't I know it! Even with my own children I have to think hard when they were born. My brothers and sisters are a bit easier, because I've known them longer. Parents are quite easy for the same reason, but when it comes to in-laws, nephews, and nieces, I really struggle. As for the birthdays of cousins, great aunts, and uncles—well I simply don't know. Oh, and I remember my wife's (on pain of death) and my own, of course. That's about it.

Come to think of it, there is one other birthday I never forget. A birthday the world has never forgotten. The birthday of Jesus. A birth so unusual and yet so normal. A birth unheralded then, but inescapable today. A first intake of breath that, silent though it may have been, has not stopped echoing around the globe from that day until the present.

There were no pictures of this birth. No announcements in the newspaper. There was no entry in a book somewhere of the surgeon or midwife. And yet that birth has caused more joy and celebration than all the world's babies put together. The simple delight of mother and father has crossed time, land, and seas and come to me, leaving a smile on my face and a skip in my heart.

What a happy birthday!

B<small>UT WHEN THE TIME HAD FULLY</small>
C<small>OME,</small> G<small>OD SENT</small> H<small>IS</small> S<small>ON, BORNE OF</small>
A <small>WOMAN, BORN UNDER LAW</small> . . .

Galatians 4:4

G<small>REAT LITTLE ONE</small>!
W<small>HOSE ALL-EMBRACING BIRTH</small>
L<small>IFTS</small> E<small>ARTH TO</small> H<small>EAVEN,</small>
S<small>TOOPS</small> H<small>EAVEN TO</small> E<small>ARTH</small>

Richard Crashaw

Every little child in all the
world has been a little safer
since the coming of the Child of
Bethlehem.

Roy L. Smith

Child in the manger,
Infant of Mary;
Outcast and stranger,
Lord of all;
Child who inherits
All our transgressions,
All our demerits
On Him fall.

Mary Macdonald

Away in a manger, no crib for a
  bed,
The little Lord Jesus laid down
  his sweet head.
The stars in the sky looked down
  where he lay,
The little Lord Jesus asleep in the
  hay.

Traditional

He Just Loves Saving

"It's just a little something I've saved up for Christmas." My grandmother's words were not entirely true. The "little something" was not that little—at least not to a child unused to seeing paper money. Nor was I the only one who received it. I had two uncles, one aunt, seven cousins, and two sisters, so the same "little something" added up for a lady whose husband had died long ago and for whom the bills seemed larger each passing year. And what she did at Christmas, she did at Easter, for birthdays, and holidays, too.

When Grandma died, and I was older, I asked my mom how her mother had been able to afford to be so generous to all her grandchildren. She shrugged her shoulders and stared out of the window. "I think she couldn't afford not to. Grandma loved to save."

Thinking of my kind, smiling grandmother helps me, in some small way, to understand why God presented the world with a "little something" He had saved for that first Christmas. He did it because He couldn't afford not to. He loved to save. Giving Jesus cost Him that is certain, but He could not, He dare not, allow men and women to pass through life unaware of His saving love.

As I think back, I realize that happy though we all were to receive crisp dollar bills from Grandma, her joy was deeper and richer. And I'm pretty sure that's how God feels too.

. . . You are to give him the name
Jesus, because he will save his
people from their sins.

Matthew 1:21

Christians awake! Salute the
  happy morn,
Whereon the Savior of mankind
  was born;
Rise to adore the mystery of
  love
Which hosts of angels chanted
  from above;
With them the joyful tidings
  first begun
Of God incarnate, of the Virgin's
  Son.

John Byrom

Hark! the herald-angels sing
Glory to the new-born King,
Peace on earth, and mercy mild,
God and sinners reconciled.

Charles Wesley

A Piece of
Christmas Peace

Where is the best place to go at Christmas time if you want a bit of peace and quiet? I'm asking because I've spent all my life looking, and I still haven't found it. I doubt if there is a single place on earth that doesn't increase in hustle and bustle in the run up to December 25th. There is scarcely room to breathe in the malls. The television blares out advertising 24/7 and when, finally, I think I'm safe and the long awaited day arrives, it is full of noise and laughter, as all manner of relatives crowd into my home.

The world is never calm at the best of times, but at Christmastime it reaches new levels of chaos and disorder. Which makes it rather ironic that the Prince of Peace should wish to come down here in the first place. He didn't have a peaceful start . . . his parents had to search hard for a place for the night. Then the visitors! All very nice, I'm sure, but they all seemed to be strangers—not a doting grandparent, aunt, or uncle in sight. Next, he had to escape to Egypt to avoid being killed and, finally, many years later, he barely had a moment to himself. And yet this busy man, this sought-after man, who was always in demand, gives the impression of being the most peaceful, calmest person the world has ever known. The unruffled eye in the middle of a violent storm.

How I wish that for once, this Christmas, I would take time to stop and come to know again that peace does not depend upon outer circumstances, but on an inner state that only the Prince of Peace can give. Please help me, God, to realize just a little piece of your peace this Christmas.

AND HE WILL BE CALLED . . . PRINCE
OF PEACE.

Isaiah 9:6

HAIL THE HEAVEN-BORN PRINCE OF
PEACE!

Charles Wesley

CHRIST BRINGS LASTING PEACE—
PEACE WITH GOD,
PEACE AMONG MEN AND NATIONS, AND
PEACE WITHIN OUR HEARTS.

Billy Graham

Hope Full

Christmas has always been a time of hope. When I was young, I hoped that it would come quickly, and when it did, all the presents I hoped for would lie around the tree in our front room. As I grew a little older, I hoped that it would snow, that the food would be good (it always was). A couple of times, I hoped to see a favorite movie, sing a favorite carol, or see a girl I liked at church.

Some people say that as you get older the magic, the excitement of Christmas fades, but I think it just changes. I still have some of the same hopes. I still like to see that movie I missed at the theater, or sing that carol. (I always get to see my favorite girl at church, only now I call her my wife.) But some of the hopes I have come from a different, and hopefully wiser, perspective. I hope Christmas comes quickly to stop the children snooping and hunting for presents. I hope that they like the presents we have bought. (OK, I confess that my favorite girl does most of the shopping.) I hope all those who eat with us enjoy the meal. It's as though my childhood hopes have . . . well, grown up and turned inside out.

And having gone through that process, I begin to see that God must have hopes for Christmas too. Hopes based not upon what He can get. (What do you give the owner of the universe for Christmas?) Not even on what He can give. But centered on our response to the present He has already given.

THE HOPES AND FEARS OF ALL THE YEARS
ARE MET IN THEE TONIGHT.

Phillips Brooks

OUR CHILDREN AWAIT CHRISTMAS PRESENTS LIKE POLITICIANS GETTING ELECTION RETURNS.

Marceline Cox

LIFE WITH CHRIST IS AN ENDLESS HOPE, WITHOUT HIM A HOPELESS END.

Anon.

I Wonder: Why?

Wonder (*noun*): a cause of astonishment or admiration; the quality of exciting, amazed admiration; rapt attention or astonishment at something awesomely mysterious or new to one's experience; a feeling of doubt or uncertainty.

I trust my dictionary, but every now and again I can't help but think that the one-dimensional words it contains sometimes need shaking and turning upside-down. It's not their fault, I suppose. A word has never woken up on Christmas morning to find its stocking full. A word has never raced downstairs to find a pile of presents underneath the Christmas tree. It has never seen its eyes in a mirror, almost popping with disbelief as it rips aside wrapping paper and discovers the very toy that had filled its dreams for weeks and weeks.

A word has never crunched the snow

beneath its feet or watched its breath cloud in the clear morning air. It has never walked to church to greet familiar faces. Nor has it heard the songs of joy and peace sung by a thousand thankful voices. A word has never sat back and listened while someone read the story of how, long ago, a baby was born. How angels, shepherds, and wise men came and worshiped. How people felt. How people still feel. How thousands have done their best to put back into the word *wonder* the experience of understanding how God once became a tiny child. What a wonder it is!

NOTHING IN FICTION IS SO FANTASTIC AS IS THIS TRUTH OF THE INCARNATION.

Jim Packer

I CANNOT TELL WHY HE WHOM
   ANGELS WORSHIP,
SHOULD SET HIS LOVE UPON THE SONS
   OF MEN,
OR WHY, AS SHEPHERD, HE SHOULD
   SEEK THE WANDERERS,
TO BRING THEM BACK, THEY KNOW
   NOT HOW OR WHEN.
BUT THIS I KNOW, THAT HE WAS BORN
   OF MARY,
WHEN BETHLEHEM'S MANGER WAS HIS
   ONLY HOME,
AND THAT HE LIVED AT NAZARETH
   AND LABORED,
AND SO THE SAVIOR, SAVIOR OF THE
   WORLD IS COME.

William Young Fullerton

. . . AND ALL WHO HEARD IT WERE
AMAZED AT WHAT THE SHEPHERDS
SAID TO THEM.

Luke 2:18

Flames of Joy

Each one of us would light a candle or two. Dad would switch out the light and Mom would start the singing. We sang quietly, concentrating more on the dancing flames and the happy faces they faintly illuminated than on the words themselves.

That's how I remember our family dinner on Christmas day, when, rather than give thanks for the food, we would sing "Away in a Manger."

And there has been many a time since when I have taken my own children in my arms and rocked them gently, singing my favorite carol in a tuneless voice. I have sat through countless church services, punctuated by coughs and whisperings that mysteriously fade away when the lullaby melody drifts through the air. And each time it takes me back, not to the first Christmas, but to the Christmases of my childhood. To those shadows. To the smiles and the power of those tiny candles, lit in the darkness. Each one kind and easy on the eye. Fragile and yet powerful. Strong and determined. Unafraid of the cold and the night. Giving everything and holding nothing in reserve.

And then I find that I have unconsciously arrived at that first Christmas.

Whether Mary and Joseph had any light in their makeshift delivery room, I don't know. What I do know is that the weak, vulnerable baby whose every movement lit up their faces with joy, had within him the light of a thousand suns and light enough for a million, million hearts.

A Christmas candle is a lovely
thing;
It makes no noise at all,
But softly gives itself away;
While quite unselfish, it grows
small.

Eva K. Logue

The true light that gives light
to every man was coming into the
world.

John 1:9

There's a song in the air!
There's a star in the sky!
There's a mother's prayer and a
baby's cry!
And the star rains its fire while
beauty sings,
For the manger at Bethlehem
cradles a King!

Josiah G. Holland

Musical Goose Bumps

No matter how hard I try, I can't find a single song in the Christmas story. Close inspection of the Gospels reveals that Mary's song, the Magnificat, was said not sung. Ditto Zechariah's when his son John the Baptist was born. Even the angels appear to have said "Glory to God," rather than splitting into four-part harmony and giving the shepherds an exclusive barber shop concert.

So why is it that we have a special name for Christmas songs? Why are there so many of them? Why do we love to hear carol singers, or venture forth ourselves to sing to complete strangers? Why do so many, who haven't sung a note for most of the year, suddenly immerse themselves in well-loved tunes, learnt in child-hood and never forgotten? What about all the

Christmas concerts and performances of masterpieces such as Handel's *Messiah?* What is the connection between the birth of Christ and our desire to sing?

Historians tell us that caroling from one house to another started during the eighteenth century or possibly earlier. Those who did this received food, money, or drink for the spreading of good cheer or *wassailing*. Dictionary editors tell us that the word carol has its origins in foreign words that carry a hint of dancing.

What these learned people fail to explain is that all carols spring from a heart and mind so excited and humbled by the facts of Christmas that, when words run out of passion and power, music alone can cause goose bumps in the soul and shivers of joy down the spine.

SING, CHOIRS OF ANGELS,
SING IN EXULTATION,
SING, ALL YE CITIZENS OF HEAVEN
ABOVE,
"GLORY TO God,
GLORY IN THE HIGHEST."

Latin, Seventeenth century

ALL PEOPLE THAT ON EARTH DO
   DWELL,
SING TO THE LORD WITH CHEERFUL
   VOICE;
HIM SERVE WITH MIRTH, HIS PRAISE
   FORTH TELL;
COME YE BEFORE HIM AND REJOICE.

William Kethe

SAID THE LITTLE LAMB TO THE
   SHEPHERD BOY
DO YOU HEAR WHAT I HEAR?
RINGING THROUGH THE SKY, SHEPHERD
   BOY
DO YOU HEAR WHAT I HEAR?
A SONG, A SONG
HIGH ABOVE THE TREES
WITH A VOICE AS BIG AS THE SEA.

Noel Regney and Gloria Shayne

Goodwill, Pass It On

"What is it this time? Not another message, surely!" "Yes, but we've got to do some editing, too. Turn it into something short and snappy."

"OK, let's have a look at the basic text then."

"Well, all of us—a heavenly host, in fact—are supposed to communicate the following: This very day a child, the only Son of the one true Creator God, has been born. His birth will affect everyone everywhere. No matter what language people speak, no matter where they live, no matter how old or young, clever or slow, married or single, it makes no difference. News of this day will speed around the world, cheering the hearts of those ready to accept it as a sign that God has not given up. Undeniable proof that He still loves and cares for all that He has made. A certain sign that He loves all people. An example of compassion for a man to pass on to his fellow man, a woman to her friends, children to their classmates. A way of life to be taken beyond the confines of those they know and passed around the globe in a chain of mercy and love made in heaven. A way of life for all of life."

"What about 'Glory to God in the highest, and on earth peace to those on whom His favor rests'?"

"Do we need to put in something about behaving in this way every day of the year?"

"No, they'll realize that, won't they?"

ALL GLORY BE TO GOD ON HIGH,
AND TO THE EARTH BE PEACE;
GOODWILL HENCEFORTH FROM HEAVEN
TO MEN
BEGIN AND NEVER CEASE.

Nahum Tate

LET US OPEN UP OUR NATURES,
THROW WIDE THE DOORS OF OUR
HEARTS, AND LET IN THE SUNSHINE OF
GOODWILL AND KINDNESS.

O. S. Marden

I Found Room for Jesus

There is a plaque outside Hodgenville, Kentucky, that marks the birthplace of Abraham Lincoln. I wonder if there ever was one outside the inn where Mary and Joseph tried to get a room? "We turned away the parents of Jesus." It's not the sort of thing you'd want to remember. Or is it? For centuries, the innkeeper has had bad press—a heartless man with no time for a pregnant woman and her anxious husband. But maybe it's time someone cut him some slack.

Everyone had been in a rush to get to Bethlehem in time for the census ordered by the Roman emperor, Caesar Augustus. Rushing is the last thing a pregnant woman wants to do. So along with Joseph, Mary slowly plods (despite the tradition, there is no hint of a donkey in the

Bible) all the way from Nazareth. It's no surprise that, when they finally get there, everyone else has beaten them to it. So what is the innkeeper to do? The easiest thing would be to shrug his shoulders, point to the "No vacancies" sign and carry on with the paperwork. Instead, he does what he can. He goes beyond the normal parameters of his work, or what that baby would later call going the second mile, and gives them a spot in the stable. And perhaps, knowing he'd done the best he could, he would one day put up a sign that proudly stated, "I found room for Jesus."

SHE WRAPPED HIM IN CLOTHS AND PLACED HIM IN A MANGER, BECAUSE THERE WAS NO ROOM FOR THEM IN THE INN.

Luke 2:7

BUT IN BETHLEHEM'S HOME THERE
 WAS FOUND NO ROOM
FOR THY HOLY NATIVITY:
O COME TO MY HEART, LORD JESUS,
THERE IS ROOM IN MY HEART FOR
 THEE.

Emily Steele Elliott

Hold Your Noses!

Each year, the children at our church act out the story of the birth of Jesus for the rest of the congregation. Moms, and maybe dads, toil for hours making angels' wings, shepherds' clothes, sheep and cattle costumes. Others patiently teach the youngsters their lines, knowing full well that on the day many will be too frightened to remember a word or scan the company come to watch so that they can wave to their grandma or next-door neighbor. No effort is spared in making the whole nativity scene as realistic as possible. You can almost close your eyes and picture yourself back in that quiet, tranquil stable all those years ago.

The trouble is that once you close your eyes, you realize that there is something missing.

All the stables and cattle sheds I have ever been in are nothing like the one at the front of the building. The noise is constant. Chickens clucking, sheep baaing, cows mooing, donkeys braying. And the smell—not to mention the fear of putting your foot in the substance that is causing it!

There's no doubt about it. Stables are not high-tech delivery suites with 24/7 medical care.

All this makes God's decision to allow His only son's first breath to be tainted by such squalor even more amazing.

ONCE IN ROYAL DAVID'S CITY
STOOD A LOWLY CATTLE SHED,
WHERE A MOTHER LAID HER BABY
IN A MANGER FOR HIS BED.

Cecil Frances Alexander

YOU WILL FIND A BABY WRAPPED IN
CLOTHS AND LYING IN A MANGER.

Luke 2:12

WHY LIES HE IN SUCH MEAN ESTATE
WHERE OX AND ASS ARE FEEDING?

Traditional

Promises, Promises

Why does some of the best food come round at Christmas time? It's as though the calorie-laden recipes are biding their time all year round, just waiting until I'm relaxing, off guard, ready to succumb to their intoxicating tastes.

"We'll get him again." "Another few notches on his belt." "It'll be easy," they say.

The sad thing is that I promised myself I would keep an eye on things. I wasn't going to overindulge. No seconds. Be thankful for one helping, and refuse all efforts to be persuaded to have a few extra mouthfuls. Last January, I decided this was going to be the Christmas I didn't put on weight. My resolve lasted all year ... until that first gift box of chocolates arrived.

Thankfully, when God says He is going to do something, His promise lasts longer than a year. Centuries before Jesus was born, He told

His people He was going to send someone to sort out their problems. Sometimes life was good, sometimes it was bad. There must have been moments when all but a few people forgot that God had made the promise in the first place. But God never forgot. It was always at the front of His mind. And when the right time came to honor the promise He had made to us humans, nothing could sway Him from it. That night Jesus was born. The fruit of a promise once made, never forgotten.

Come, Thou long-expected Jesus,
Born to set Thy people free;
From our fears and sins release
  us;
Let us find our rest in Thee.

Charles Wesley

God's promises are, virtually, obligations that He imposes upon Himself.

Friedrich Wilhelm Krummacher

God is the God of promise.

Colin Urquhart

A Favorite Carol

Christmas carols are like a favorite treat—a musical chocolate box—full of old familiar tastes. As they come round, the memory of past indulgences wanders through the heart, calling us to reflect again upon this magical time of year. They are as comfortable as an old friend who has been away on a year-long journey, and as new and interesting as the tales he or she comes to tell us.

While I don't have a favorite, there is one that I feel I have to sing on Christmas day itself. "O Come All Ye Faithful," translated from the original Latin by Frederick Oakley in the nineteenth century, somehow captures for me the joy of Christmas. It reminds me to turn my eyes from the now that I can see, to the past I cannot. It bids me cross to Bethlehem, the middle of nowhere, the center of everywhere. It focuses my concentration on the one true eternal God and His Son, stepping down from the infinite to wear the clothes of the finite.

It reminds me that what many people could not see, cannot now see, and will never see is as obvious to the angels as the nose on their face— or whatever phrase those heavenly beings use to describe the glaringly obvious.

But best of all, it allows me, though I'm not a shepherd, a wise man (no comment on that one), a Mary, or a Joseph, to welcome God's final word to humanity into the world.

Yea, Lord *I* greet Thee
Born this happy morning.

O COME, ALL YE FAITHFUL,
JOYFUL AND TRIUMPHANT,
O COME YE, O COME YE TO
   BETHLEHEM;
COME AND BEHOLD HIM,
BORN THE KING OF ANGELS:
O COME, LET US ADORE HIM, CHRIST
   THE LORD.

Latin, Seventeenth century

I HEARD THE BELLS ON CHRISTMAS
DAY
THEIR OLD FAMILIAR CAROLS PLAY,
AND WILD AND SWEET
THE WORDS REPEAT
OF PEACE ON EARTH, GOODWILL TO
MEN!

Henry Wadsworth Longfellow

CHRISTMAS IS THE DAY THAT HOLDS
ALL TIME TOGETHER.

Alexander Smith

SOMEONE BEGAN TO SING, "COME, ALL
YE FAITHFUL." I JOINED IN AND SANG
WITH THE STRANGERS ALL ABOUT ME.
I AM NOT ALONE AT ALL, I THOUGHT. I
WAS NEVER ALONE AT ALL. AND THAT, OF
COURSE, IS THE MESSAGE OF
CHRISTMAS. WE ARE NEVER ALONE.
NOT WHEN THE NIGHT IS DARKEST, THE
WIND COLDEST, THE WORLD SEEMINGLY
MOST INDIFFERENT. FOR THIS IS STILL
THE TIME GOD CHOOSES.

Taylor Caldwell

In a Word

This Christmas will be full of words. Greetings by word of mouth. You've taken the words right out of my mouth. Upon my word, that is a great present! He's a man of few words. I promise, on my word of honor, not to drink too much. Yes, I will play that word-association game. Not in so many words, no. Many a true word spoken in jest. I hope my manager put in a good word for me in the annual pay review. Santa was as good as his word again. Famous last words. Clever play on words, that. Have you seen the new word-processing package I got? Why won't you take me at my word? You remembered that speech word for word. This is the last word in computer technology. If she continues to behave like that, someone is going to have to have words with her. Cold is not the word for it, it's freezing! A picture paints a thousand words. Look at the nice words on this Christmas card. This will make you eat your words. In other words. Words fail me. Not in so many words, no. Come on, Granddad, say a few words. I can't put my feelings for you into words. Trust Uncle Robert to have the last word. You can eat when I give the word. He'll do it, he is a man of his word. Have a quiet word in her ear, will you? Actions speak louder than words.

Surely that covers everything. There's no need to say another word. What's that you say? I've left one out?

Oh yes.

Jesus, the Word of God.

The Word became flesh and made his dwelling among us.

John 1:14

Word of the Father, Now in flesh appearing: O come, let us adore Him, Christ the Lord.

Latin, Seventeenth century

. . . But in these last days He has spoken to us by His Son . . .

Hebrews 1:2

Like Father,
Like Son

Ooh, it's a boy. You must be so proud. When did the waters break? One, two, three, four, five, six, seven, eight, nine, ten. Yes, ten fingers. What are you going to call him? Don't hold him like that. Try and get your arm underneath to support his head. You must be tired. Can I get you something? How long were you in labor? Were you at the birth, too? What about feeding? You know they need something every two, three, four hours. Look, I've knitted a little something. That ought to keep him warm. Can I hold him? Ooh, isn't he lovely! I just love the way he gurgles. I always used to feed them and then rock them on my shoulder for a bit just to get rid of the . . . you know . . . the wind. Oops, there goes some now. Oh! Now he's got the hiccups. Poor little thing. Doesn't he look sweet when he screws his nose up like that? So what are you going to call him? Listen. Now he's gurgling. That's the sign of a contented baby. Does he sleep well? That's all they want to do really, isn't it? Sleep and eat. They always look so innocent. He's worth the wait, isn't he? Just turn him over on his side when he does that. I'm just trying to work out who he's like.

He's got his mother's eyes and nose, but if I'm perfectly honest I'd have to say . . . I think he's just like his Father.

CHRISTMAS IS THE GIFT FROM
   HEAVEN
OF GOD'S SON GIVEN FOR FREE;
IF CHRISTMAS ISN'T FOUND IN YOUR
   HEART,
YOU WON'T FIND IT UNDER THE TREE.

Charlotte Carpenter

SILENT NIGHT, HOLY NIGHT!
SON OF GOD, O HOW BRIGHT
LOVE IS SMILING FROM THY FACE!
STRIKES FOR US NOW THE HOUR OF
   GRACE,
SAVIOR, SINCE THOU ART BORN,
SAVIOR, SINCE THOU ART BORN.

Joseph Mohr

. . . JESUS CHRIST HIS ONLY SON OUR
LORD, WHO WAS CONCEIVED BY THE
HOLY GHOST, BORN OF THE VIRGIN
MARY . . .

Apostles' Creed

When I'm Older

"Can you see who it is at the door, Joseph?"

"Hello, do I know you . . . any of you?"

"Er . . . em . . . you probably think we're a bit crazy, but an angel just told us to come and see the baby. There is a baby here, isn't there?"

"Of course . . ."

"Who is it, dear?"

"Oh, just some shepherds."

Why shepherds? Why not a mother-in-law, a sister, or a cousin? Why did God send an angel to tell shepherds to be the first people to see the baby Jesus? Was it because they happened to be the nearest available humans and God, like any parent, was dying to tell someone of the birth of His son? Unlikely. After all, the innkeeper or the guests at his inn would have been closer.

It's more to do with the fact that they were

. . . well, shepherds. These men made their living performing an antisocial job. They lived out in the fields, in all weathers. They were rough-and-ready sort of people, not the sort most would want at their social gatherings. Outsiders, strangers, the sort of people who arouse suspicion, not respect.

God was making a statement. He had sent His son to those on the fringes, the left-outs, the excluded. They were the ones who would be attracted to Him, while the decent people would remain disinterested and superior. And when Mary would tell him about those first visitors, it wouldn't surprise me if Jesus' heart skipped a beat and he whispered to himself, "I'm going to be a shepherd when I grow up."

WHILE SHEPHERDS WATCHED THEIR
  FLOCKS BY NIGHT,
ALL SEATED ON THE GROUND,
THE ANGEL OF THE LORD CAME
  DOWN,
AND GLORY SHONE AROUND.

Nahum Tate

AND THERE WERE SHEPHERDS
LIVING OUT IN THE FIELDS NEARBY,
KEEPING WATCH OVER THEIR FLOCKS
AT NIGHT.

Luke 2:8

WHAT CAN I GIVE HIM,
POOR AS I AM!
IF I WERE A SHEPHERD
I WOULD BRING A LAMB;
IF I WERE A WISE MAN,
I WOULD DO MY PART;
YET WHAT I CAN I GIVE HIM—
GIVE MY HEART.

Christina Rossetti

Eternal Joy

I've just come back from the most remarkable scientific expedition. You see, I had made a "joyometer." A device for measuring the joy in any person at any given moment in time. To test it out, I jumped back into the pages of the Bible around the time when Jesus was born. The results were pretty much as I expected:

Elizabeth the mother of John the Baptist scored well, as did John himself. Even though he was still in his mother's womb, he managed a pretty high reading when Mary came near.

Mary herself did well. The pointer on the instrument rocketed sky high when she was holding Jesus in her arms. That's a mom for you! Naturally, Joseph was high too, in a silent, fatherly sort of way. The shepherds weren't quite so high—I suppose they've seen enough births with their lambs and such. The Wise Men notched up a good reading, not as high as

I'd expected, but then they were a bit worn out with the traveling and everything. Of course, when I showed it to Herod, the arrow stopped dead and didn't move an inch. Nothing unusual there!

As far as the angels were concerned, I couldn't get a clear result, although it seemed to be pretty high. There were too many of them and they wouldn't stay still. Actually, to be honest, they frightened me a bit and I was shaking so much that I couldn't keep the instrument steady. When they disappeared, I decided enough was enough.

But just as I was getting ready to come back, something strange took place. No one was about and I just happened to point the "joyometer" toward heaven. You'll never believe what happened next. The reading shot off the scale, and the whole thing exploded.

JOY TO THE WORLD! THE LORD IS
  COME;
LET EARTH RECEIVE HER KING.

Isaac Watts

I BRING YOU GOOD NEWS OF GREAT
JOY THAT WILL BE FOR ALL THE
PEOPLE.

Luke 2:10

GREAT JOYS, LIKE GRIEFS, ARE
SILENT.

Shackerley Marmion

Spot the Star

Once, when I was younger, I was lying on a beach in France staring at the evening sky. It was July 14, Bastille Day, an annual holiday. Some thoughtful people in the local authority had organized a spectacular fireworks display. Each time a rocket soared upwards and exploded in a shower of color, the crowd "oohed" and "aahed" in amazement. For thirty stunning minutes the display continued, increasing in crescendo to the grand finale, after which the satisfied spectators slipped away, chattering contentedly. I remained, my eyes slowly adjusting to the natural darkness. There was no sound except the lazy rise and fall of the waves against the sand. I was the only one who noticed the other lights in the sky. Bigger, older, brighter, and a million times more wonderful than the temporary flashes that had distracted so many for all of half an hour. And I thought how human the crowd had been. How typical of us to have been amused by fireworks when the real things were twinkling patiently all along.

At the top of my Christmas tree shines a golden star, feebly reflecting the artificial light of the nearest lamp. We all know it is just cardboard inside, but it looks nice, and we'd rather have it there than a fairy or anything else. But it's not a patch on the star that made those Wise Men sit up and think. Think and travel. Travel and worship. Worship and give. What a sight that must have been! That is my kind of star!

But wait a minute! Now who's being shallow? Wasn't something . . . or someone else there, bigger, older, brighter, and a million times more wonderful than the object those Wise Men followed?

O STAR OF WONDER, STAR OF LIGHT,
STAR WITH ROYAL BEAUTY BRIGHT,
WESTWARD LEADING, STILL
  PROCEEDING,
GUIDE US TO THY PERFECT LIGHT.

John H. Hopkins

B RIGHT STAR, WOULD I WERE
STEADFAST AS THOU ART.

John Keats

W E SAW HIS STAR IN THE EAST AND
HAVE COME TO WORSHIP HIM.

Matthew 2:2

S TAR OF THE EAST, THOU HOPE OF
  THE SOUL
OH STAR THAT LEADS TO GOD ABOVE
WHOSE RAYS ARE PEACE AND JOY AND
  LOVE
WATCH O'ER US STILL TILL LIFE HATH
  CEASED
BEAM ON, BRIGHT STAR, SWEET
  BETHLEHEM STAR.

George Cooper

The Foolish Wise Men

At first glance, the Wise Men of the Christmas story seem anything but wise. They are watching the sky, and one day they notice a new star. So what do they decide to do? Follow it. All the way from the security and comfort of their homes in some unknown eastern land to Jerusalem.

Then what do they do? They go to the ruler of the land and ask him where a new king has been born. Hardly the most sensible thing to say to a power-crazy monarch. And if they were good at understanding stars, they don't seem to have been too hot at understanding people. They fail to note Herod's pretense about wanting to see the new baby, and it is only thanks to divine intervention that they are prevented from returning and giving him just the information he needed to kill Jesus.

It's difficult to find much wisdom in any of these actions.

And yet, one thing demonstrates beyond a shadow of doubt that they were indeed wise men. One act that shows how sensible they really were. Behavior that is the summit of human wisdom. Higher and better and more insightful than the thoughts and words and deeds of the greatest philosopher and deepest thinker the world has ever known.

So what is it that makes them worthy bearers of the name wise?

When they came face to face with the Christmas child, they bowed down and worshiped him.

WE THREE KINGS OF ORIENT ARE;
BEARING GIFTS WE TRAVERSE AFAR,
FIELD AND FOUNTAIN, MOOR AND
    MOUNTAIN,
FOLLOWING YONDER STAR.

John H. Hopkins

WE SAW HIS STAR IN THE EAST AND
HAVE COME TO WORSHIP HIM.

Matthew 2:2

OUR GREATEST CLAIM TO NOBILITY
IS OUR CREATED CAPACITY TO KNOW
GOD, TO BE IN PERSONAL
RELATIONSHIP WITH HIM, TO LOVE
HIM, AND TO WORSHIP HIM. INDEED,
WE ARE MOST TRULY HUMAN WHEN
WE ARE ON OUR KNEES BEFORE OUR
CREATOR.

John R. W. Stott

CHRISTMAS IN BETHLEHEM. THE
ANCIENT DREAM: A COLD, CLEAR
NIGHT MADE BRILLIANT BY A GLORIOUS
STAR, THE SMELL OF INCENSE,
SHEPHERDS AND WISE MEN FALLING TO
THEIR KNEES IN ADORATION OF THE
SWEET BABY, THE INCARNATION OF
PERFECT LOVE.

Lucinda Franks

Over the Moon

A theology student, when presented with a Greek copy of Matthew chapter 2, once translated the tenth verse in this way. "When they (the Wise Men) saw the star, they were over the moon." I don't know whether the examiner gave him a good mark or not, but I think his phrasing helps explain why they did what they did next: They went into a house and saw the person they had been trying to track down. Then, great, wealthy, and important people though they undoubtedly were, they dropped to their knees and worshiped a child they had never seen before.

They had found what they had been looking for. The discovery of the object of their quest filled them with many emotions. They were beside themselves with excitement and anticipation. The Wise Men experienced that moment of satisfaction, that "this is it" sensation when the goal is in sight, within touching distance.

When the mountain has been climbed and all that is needed is to turn round and enjoy the fullness of a view long anticipated.

But their joy was not yet complete. It was still bottled up, contained within themselves. Beneath the surface, it was waiting to erupt and spill over. What they needed was to release it. And when they saw the object itself—Himself—it flowed out in the only way it knew. In the only way it could. In worship.

First they saw the star, then the Son. And they were still over the moon.

ON COMING TO THE HOUSE, THEY SAW THE CHILD WITH HIS MOTHER MARY, AND THEY BOWED DOWN AND WORSHIPED HIM.

Matthew 2:11

IT IS ONLY WHEN MEN BEGIN TO WORSHIP THAT THEY BEGIN TO GROW.

Calvin Coolidge

O COME, LET US ADORE HIM, CHRIST THE LORD.

Latin, seventeenth century

Saying Thank You

I didn't mean to get angry. I only meant to show him that I was sad. My son forgot to say "thank you" for the present we had bought him. We had warned him to thank grandparents, uncles, and aunts for every gift—whether he liked it or not. We just assumed he would thank us for the new toy he had been nagging us about for the last few months. But he didn't. And it felt like he was taking us for granted. Not even his genuine joy for a wanted present could take away our feelings of . . . well, of having been left out.

And now I can't help wonder if sometimes God feels the same way. Millions and millions of people so absorbed in unwrapping their presents . . . trying them on and trying them out, that they forget to say thank you to the great Giver. The giver of a small child. The giver of love. The giver of life.

I wonder if God gets cross? Or perhaps, like

me, He just feels left out. All the fun of the party, and so many people have forgotten about Him. Amidst all the "Oh, you shouldn't have," the "It's just what I wanted," and the "It's great. . . . what is it?" is He looking down on our joy and quietly waiting? Waiting for those simple words. Thank you.

> GIVE THANKS WITH A GRATEFUL
> HEART,
> GIVE THANKS TO THE HOLY ONE.
> GIVE THANKS BECAUSE HE'S GIVEN
> JESUS CHRIST HIS SON.
>
> *Henry Smith*

> O LORD! THAT LENDS ME LIFE,
> LEND ME A HEART REPLETE WITH
> THANKFULNESS!
>
> *William Shakespeare*

> THANKSGIVING PUTS POWER INTO
> LIVING, BECAUSE IT OPENS THE
> GENERATORS OF THE HEART TO
> RESPOND GRATEFULLY, TO RECEIVE
> JOYFULLY, AND TO REACT CREATIVELY.
>
> *C. Neil Strait*

And the Two Shall Become a Family

There is something special about Christmas when there is a child in a house for the first time. What was once a couple has wonderfully become a family, and through the arrival of a baby, the parents become young again and remember the happy days of their own childhood. The extravagances, the decorations, the fun, and the laughter can all be justified in the name of the infant. Grandparents, uncles, aunts, and cousins join in as the child sleeps, wakes, eats, and sleeps oblivious to much of the excitement going on around her.

Christmas time is family time. Not because of what you or I do. Not because of what your parents and my parents did. It is because one special couple became a family in a Bethlehem stable. They may not have had the luxuries we have today. They certainly weren't in their own home. The best they could get was a borrowed manger. There were no holiday treats, no turkey. No cards hung up on the walls. No mailman bringing them boxes to shake and guess over. No carols, no trip to church, no anticipation of the post-Christmas sales, no trees, no Santa Claus.

And yet they seemed to get along fine with what they had. They were far from home, overwhelmed by the circumstances that had swept over them in the previous months. Away from the familiar, facing the daunting prospect of surviving in a disturbing world. And yet they had one thing that first Christmas. Perhaps the best thing anyone can ever have. They had each other. They were a family.

CHRISTMAS IS THE SEASON OF JOY,
OF HOLIDAY GREETINGS EXCHANGED,
OF GIFT GIVING, AND OF FAMILIES
UNITED.

Norman Vincent Peale

CHRISTMAS IS A DAY OF MEANING
AND TRADITIONS, A SPECIAL DAY
SPENT IN THE WARM CIRCLE OF
FAMILY AND FRIENDS.

Margaret Thatcher

AT CHRISTMAS ALL ROADS LEAD
HOME.

Marjorie Holmes

Coping with Disappointment

I t's time to open the presents. Great, I've got the book I've dreamed of, the CD of my favorite band, but is that it? What about . . . what I've been longing for?

Christmas does bring its excitement, but it seems to bring disappointment too. Great games—but "batteries not included," so that you can't play with the action toy. Or your parents get you the wrong toy (surely they must know which ones you've got already). Or worse still, you don't even get the big one, the present you've been dropping hints about since way back in the summer. (A colleague still remembers, forty years on, that he never got the train set he longed for.)

What do we do with these disappointments? Try to pretend they aren't there? Christmas is a bit like a vacation: After it's all over, and when you get back to work and colleagues ask if you had a good time, then the only answer that you can give is: "Yes." Once I tried saying, "It was all right," and got so many funny looks that it just wasn't worth it.

But what do we do with these disappointments in our heart? We can't deny that we do feel let down. The Christian message, the Christmas message, is that God is big enough to take care of our disappointments. We don't have to pretend to Him that everything is hunky-dory when it plainly isn't. We can share our lives fully with our maker. We may feel *let down* but we can *let in* our Lord. We can share our feelings with Him. We can open up our hearts to Jesus Christ. He understands. He cares. He knows.

How about trying it?

O COME TO MY HEART, LORD JESUS
THERE IS ROOM IN MY HEART FOR
  THEE.

Emily Steele Elliott

THERE IS ONE SOURCE OF POWER
THAT IS STRONGER THAN EVERY
DISAPPOINTMENT, BITTERNESS, OR
INGRAINED MISTRUST, AND THAT
POWER IS JESUS CHRIST, WHO
BROUGHT FORGIVENESS AND
RECONCILIATION TO THE WORLD.

John Paul II

THE BEST WAY TO AVOID FATIGUE,
PANIC, OR DEPRESSION IS TO TRY TO
KEEP IN MIND THAT CHRISTMAS IS
INTENDED AS A CELEBRATION, NOT A
CONTEST.

Sandra Boynton

CHRISTMAS IS A GOOD TIME TO TAKE
STOCK OF OUR BLESSINGS.

Pat Boone

Absence Makes the Heart Grow Fonder

I hate removing Christmas decorations. It's not just the fact that the floor around the tree is covered in pine needles, or that when we carry it outside showers of little green arrows fall off every time we bump into something. It's the bareness. The dullness. The return to normality. The final proof, if one was really needed, that Christmas is over for another year. Eyes that have become accustomed to the color and warmth of baubles, stars, and paper chains, must now refocus on naked walls devoid of fun and joy.

It is only when the decorations are down that I begin again to realize how much I love Christmas. How good it has been to see friends and family. What fun we have had sharing meals and presents. The joy that has come into my heart as I remember the birth of Jesus. The laughter, the happiness, the peace, and the wonder of that time, which like no other, brings out the best in people all around the world.

And I wonder if perhaps the true value of decorations lies not in their presence but in their removal and absence? The space they leave reminds me of all those things I now miss and gives me a quiet resolve to make the next Christmas better than the one just gone.

DECK THE HALLS WITH BOUGHS OF HOLLY,
FA LA LA LA LA, LA LA LA LA.
'TIS THE SEASON TO BE JOLLY,
FA LA LA LA LA, LA LA LA LA.

Traditional

NEVER WORRY ABOUT THE SIZE OF YOUR CHRISTMAS TREE. IN THE EYES OF CHILDREN, THEY ARE ALL 30 FEET TALL.

Larry Wilde

CHRISTMAS IS NOT IN TINSEL AND LIGHTS AND OUTWARD SHOW . . . THE SECRET LIES IN AN INNER GLOW.

Wilfred A. Peterson

Unwanted Presents

Everybody gets Christmas presents they don't want. Not just the classics like socks, perfume, last year's must-have toy, or the ideal gift for the age you were when a distant cousin last saw you. Then there are those that are the right idea, but the wrong make, or a cheaper version of the very piece of electronic gadgetry you had just about saved up for. And finally there are those for which we say, "Thank you," but think, "When am I ever going to use that?"

Once my mother gave me just such a present. It was a briefcase. Strong and robust with plenty of useful compartments and clips for every conceivable item of stationery. The only problem was I neither wanted it or needed it. At least not for several years. It just lay in a cupboard in my room until I got a job where I had to travel around with bits of paper, documents, and literature. My briefcase and I have never looked back. Since then, it has helped me on many occasions and, as I write, it stares at me with doglike devotion, nestled within sight of my desk. Less shiny, less pristine, but more useful and more appreciated than ever in the past.

Sometimes I am tempted to think that a baby born a long time ago in a land far away is the sort of gift for which I can politely say, "Thank you" but really wonder, "When am I ever going to use that?" If so, I hope my briefcase will sneak next to my chair and trip me up when I try to leave.

HE CAME TO THAT WHICH WAS HIS
OWN, BUT HIS OWN DID NOT RECEIVE
HIM.

John 1:11

CHRISTMAS IS THE DAY WHEN ANY
GIFT, HOWEVER SMALL, SHOULD BE
GRATEFULLY RECEIVED, PROVIDED IT
IS GIVEN WITH LOVE.

Clare Boothe Luce

YOU CAN NEVER TRULY ENJOY
CHRISTMAS UNTIL YOU CAN LOOK UP
INTO THE FATHER'S FACE AND TELL
HIM YOU HAVE RECEIVED HIS
CHRISTMAS GIFT.

John R. Rice

Just a Normal Baby

What sort of baby was Jesus? If you look at some of the well-known Christmas songs, you see their authors were divided on the matter. In one well-known carol, we are encouraged to think that, although Jesus was woken up by the noise of cattle, for some reason he didn't cry or scream in any way. Yet, in another equally loved one we are informed that Jesus was exactly like us. For, just as we did when we were little, he knew the pleasure of smiles and the pain of tears.

I have to confess, as a parent, my money is on the second one.

Of course, it may have been that baby Jesus never cried to be fed or squealed in fear or delight. His face may never have gone red with effort when emptying his bowels. He may never have tripped when learning to walk, or been unable to pronounce his own name properly at first. Being the special baby that he was, his heavenly Father could have spared him all of these indignities of life.

But when I think of how his life ended, I realize that these were not humiliations at all. For the indignity lies not in how this innocent child behaved, but in how the guilty men and women reacted to his love and his kindness. It is found in the way they screamed and cried to have the Christmas child crucified. And even then his Father, though He could have spared him in an instant, preferred to rescue others instead.

THE HEAVENLY BABE YOU THERE
SHALL FIND
TO HUMAN VIEW DISPLAYED.
ALL MEANLY WRAPPED IN SWADDLING
BANDS,
AND IN A MANGER LAID.

Nahum Tate

Read the Small Print

Have you ever seen a Christmas card with a picture of King Herod on it? Or wrapping paper showing cruel men carrying out his orders to kill all the male children under two years of age in the Bethlehem area? I doubt it. We prefer Christmas thoughts and ideas that are kinder on the eyes and easier on the hearts. Yet, there once was a man who was not as keen as you or I on Christmas. A man who recognized the baby King as a threat to his reign, to his world. A man who would stop at nothing to thwart God's plan. Someone who didn't think for a second about the parents who would never see their boys grow up. Someone who had cunning, but not compassion, cruelty but not consideration.

Herod pretended he wanted to worship the baby that the Wise Men told him about. But it was a pack of lies. All he was interested in was murder. Only the special intervention of God prevented the death of Jesus in what we sometimes call the Massacre of the Innocents.

Suddenly, we realize that amid the story of bold-printed love and grace, joy and wonder, there is the small print. There are people. Human beings who have no interest in the coming of a child—other than trying to get rid of him, ignore him, and push him out of their world.

Welcome to our world, baby Jesus. Thank you, that you can make a difference.

HEROD THEN WITH FEAR WAS FILLED:
"A PRINCE," HE SAID, "IN JEWRY!"
ALL THE LITTLE BOYS HE KILLED
AT BETHLEHEM IN HIS FURY.

Fifteenth-century carol

. . . AND HE GAVE ORDERS TO KILL
ALL THE BOYS IN BETHLEHEM AND ITS
VICINITY WHO WERE TWO YEARS OLD
AND UNDER . . .

Matthew 2:16

The Great Escape

For a few hours once a year, we can leave the harsh, unforgiving world with its problems, its chores, its difficulties, and its worries. Safe in the harbor of our homes, we are able to gently float alongside family and friends. Loving and giving, sharing and caring. The news drifts silently by on our television screens, uninteresting and unnoticed, for the only news that matters is who gave what, who laughed when, whose jokes were the worst, who remembered last year's gathering, and who took the last helping.

The cost of the food, drinks, and presents lurks far away, blinking relentless, unobserved on some computer that couldn't get the time off. Even plans for next year's holiday lie quiet, our minds slipping more easily and comfortably to the past than to the future.

Christmas is the moment of the great

escape. When the world stops and forgets itself. That time when we can escape the mundane and the pressure of our everyday lives and rediscover the extraordinary, the inexplicable—almost anything we choose.

Some might ask, "Is it right to run away and ignore the tragedies and injustices of the world? Is it good to escape in this way?" That first Christmas, Jesus and his family escaped. On the command of an angel, they raced to Egypt out of harm's way.

But there came a time when flight was not an option. When Jesus looked death in the eye and stood his ground. Why? To allow us the way out of sin and its control, from death and its terror. So, although at Christmas we might escape for just a while, the birth of Jesus makes us aware we can escape forever.

CHRISTMAS IS OVER AND BUSINESS
IS BUSINESS.

Franklin Pierce Adams

"GET UP," HE SAID, "TAKE THE
CHILD AND HIS MOTHER AND ESCAPE
TO EGYPT."

Matthew 2:13

CHRISTMAS MAKES THE REST OF THE
YEAR WORTHWHILE.

Charles Schulz

Christmas II

Everybody talks about that First Christmas. The night when Jesus was born. The night when the couple incredibly became a family through the arrival of a baby. But does anyone ever say anything about the second Christmas? What was it like? Did Mary and Joseph become young again? Did they hang up decorations? Did they get out the photos? Were there comments like, "And what about the shepherds?" or "I'll never forget the look on your face when the Wise Men knocked on the door!" Can you imagine Joseph crawling on the floor trying to get Jesus to look at the present and forget the wooden spoon he kept banging on the floor! Is it likely that Mary presented them all with her grandmother's special recipe of plum pudding or roast goose?

Maybe one or two of those things took place, but I'm pretty sure most of them didn't.

(I'm dead sure about the photos.) Will we ever know what happened?

Of course we will. For the simple reason that Mary and Joseph were just like us. What do we do a year after a child is born? We feel happy, proud, honored, delighted, light-headed. Our hearts fill with joy, gratitude, and love. We sing songs, we give presents, we laugh, and we remember. We celebrate.

And since then, there has not been a single year when someone, somewhere has not danced for joy and celebrated at the birth of the child who was one-year-old that second Christmas.

COME AND JOIN THE CELEBRATION,
IT'S A VERY SPECIAL DAY.
COME AND SHARE OUR JUBILATION,
THERE'S A NEW KING BORN TODAY.

Valerie Collison

Good Christian men, rejoice
With heart and soul and voice;
Give ye heed to what we say,
Jesus Christ is born today:
Ox and ass before Him bow,
And He is in the manger now.
Christ is born today!

J. M. Neale

The shepherds returned,
glorifying and praising God for
all the things they had heard
and seen, which were just as they
had been told.

Luke 2:20

The light of the world is
reborn in His glory at the same
season every year. Let us bless
each other and be joyful.

Katherine Anne Porter

The Birth of Love

No one has ever seen love.

But we have observed a young girl's humble smile as she talks with an angel. We have seen an engaged man protect his fiancée from humiliation and disgrace. We have seen a mother wrap her firstborn son in simple cloths and place him gently in a manger. We have watched hard shepherds, their hearts softened by angels' wings and the sight of a tiny baby, tell all those who were prepared to listen about their wonderful night out on the hills. We have even peeped into palaces to overhear wise men speak of their journey across many miles following a star. And we have seen them lay expensive presents at the feet of a child. We have seen this child grow to a young boy, only to disappear from the public eye for many years.

We have looked again to discover him healing the sick, curing the deaf and blind, delighting the simple folk with his unpretentious wisdom and easy-to-listen-to common sense as he talked of God in ways they could understand. We have seen young and old, rulers and commoners, good and bad talk with him. We have seen him cry, we have heard him pray, we have felt him touch, we have eaten with him, and smelled the fish stink in the summer sun.

We have watched the corners of his mouth curl upwards in a smile, and we have counted the furrows on his brow as each line reflects a sorrow deeply felt and borne alone.

We have blinked as he was bathed in glory, and we have strained our eyes as he has strolled along the water as if it were a sandy path. We have heard him silent and unflinching. We have heard his anguish and solitude. We have seen him die.

I was wrong.

We have seen love.

CHRISTMAS IS A BIG LOVE AFFAIR TO
REMOVE THE WRINKLES OF THE YEAR
WITH KINDLY REMEMBRANCES.

John Wanamaker

CHRISTMAS IS THE SEASON FOR
KINDLING THE FIRE OF HOSPITALITY
IN THE HALL, THE GENIAL FLAME OF
CHARITY IN THE HEART.

Washington Irving

LOVE CAME DOWN AT CHRISTMAS,
LOVE ALL LOVELY, LOVE DIVINE;
LOVE WAS BORN AT CHRISTMAS,
STAR AND ANGELS GAVE THE SIGN.

Christina Rossetti

Andrew Bianchi is a writer who has written several books that creatively help people read the Bible. His has written a number of books, including: *The What If? Bible*; *The Truth About Ruth And Other Stories In Rhyme*; *Bible Stories*; and *The Ultimate Bible Fact and Quiz Book*.

Martin H. Manser is a reference-book editor who has written many English dictionaries and edited books that encourage Bible reading. His publications include: *Good Word Guide* (Bloomsbury); *Students' Dictionary* (Macmillan); *Dictionary of Proverbs* (Facts On File); *The Dictionary of Bible Themes* (Zondervan); *NRSV Cross-Reference Bible* (Oxford University Press); and *I Never Knew That Was in the Bible* (Nelson).